MW01104907

Daniel Buruke Weldekidan

Mitigating DoS and DDoS

with Special Emphasis on Application Layer Attacks

AV Akademikerverlag

Impressum / Imprint

Bibliografische Information der Deutschen Nationalbibliothek· Die Deutsche Nationalbibliothek verzeichnet diese Publikation in der Deutschen Nationalbibliografie; detaillierte bibliografische Daten sind im Internet über http://dnb.d-nb.de abrufbar.
Alle in diesem Buch genannten Marken und Produktnamen unterliegen warenzeichen-, marken- oder patentrechtlichem Schutz bzw. sind Warenzeichen oder eingetragene Warenzeichen der jeweiligen Inhaber. Die Wiedergabe von Marken, Produktnamen, Gebrauchsnamen, Handelsnamen, Warenbezeichnungen u.s.w. in diesem Werk berechtigt auch ohne besondere Kennzeichnung nicht zu der Annahme, dass solche Namen im Sinne der Warenzeichen- und Markenschutzgesetzgebung als frei zu betrachten wären und daher von jedermann benutzt werden dürften.

Bibliographic information published by the Deutsche Nationalbibliothek: The Deutsche Nationalbibliothek lists this publication in the Deutsche Nationalbibliografie; detailed bibliographic data are available in the Internet at http://dnb.d-nb.de.
Any brand names and product names mentioned in this book are subject to trademark, brand or patent protection and are trademarks or registered trademarks of their respective holders. The use of brand names, product names, common names, trade names, product descriptions etc. even without a particular marking in this work is in no way to be construed to mean that such names may be regarded as unrestricted in respect of trademark and brand protection legislation and could thus be used by anyone.

Coverbild / Cover image: www.ingimage.com

Verlag / Publisher:
AV Akademikerverlag
ist ein Imprint der / is a trademark of
OmniScriptum GmbH & Co. KG
Heinrich-Böcking-Str. 6-8, 66121 Saarbrücken, Deutschland / Germany
Email: info@akademikerverlag.de

Herstellung: siehe letzte Seite /
Printed at: see last page
ISBN: 978-3-639-72939-9

Copyright © 2014 OmniScriptum GmbH & Co. KG
Alle Rechte vorbehalten. / All rights reserved. Saarbrücken 2014

Table of Contents

LIST OF FIGURES

ABBREVIATIONS

ACK   Acknowledgement

ADC   Application Delivery Controller

CAPTCHA   Completely Automated Public Turing test to tell Computers and
            Humans Apart)

CERTs   Computer Emergency Response Teams

CPU   Central Processing Unit

CRS   Core Rule Set

DDoS   Distributed Denial of Service

DNS   Domain Name System

DoS   Denial of Service

DUC   Dynamic DNS Update Client

FTP   File Transfer Protocol

GBPS   Gigabytes per second

HTTP   Hypertext Transfer Protocol

ICMP   Internet Control Message Protocol

ICT   Information and Communication Technology

IDS   Intrusion Detection Systems

INI   Initialization

IT   Information Technology

LOIC   Low Orbit Ion Cannon

OS   Operating System

OSCE   Organization for Security and Co-operation in Europe

OSI	Open Systems Interconnection
OWASP	Open Web Application Security Project
PID	Process Identifier
SAL	Service Level Agreement
SMTP	Simple Mail Transfer Protocol
SQL	Structured Query Language
SRC	Source
SSYN	Slave Synchronization
SYN	Synchronization
TCP	Transmission Control Protocol
UDP	User Datagram Protocol
URL	Uniform Resource Locator
USB	Universal Serial Bus
WAF	Web Application Firewall

ABSTRACT

Denial of Service (DoS) and Distributed Denial of Service (DDoS) are among the most common threats to IT security. As it does not require advanced resources, such attacks can be carried out by private individuals as well as organized groups, so-called "hacktivists". This thesis gives an overview and detailed description of the different kind of attacks commonly used by hackers and shows the challenges for IT security experts. In a practical application exercise, a DoS attack simulation is created by using three clients with the Ubuntu 14.04 LTS operating system. One client is the attacker running the tool Low Orbit Ion Canon (LOIC), the second one is the target running an Apache 2 server, and the last one is a normal user to access the service provided by the Apache 2 server. By using these clients, an application layer HTTP flood attack is performed on the Apache 2 server. A Wireshark network utility tool is used to capture and analyze the difference between the traffic sent from the LOIC client and the normal user. In addition, a Glance tool is used to analyze how the resources of the server are affected by the attack.

In a next step, a DDoS attack is simulated with two personal computers (PC). The first PC is running the MeTUs Delphi 2.8 tool. The detailed prerequisite configurations, which are needed to create a virus using Metus Delphi, such as PortForwarding and setting up a Dynamic DNS Update Client, is shown. The second PC is used to run the virus created and is compromised to become part of the botnet. Then, a SSYN attack is carried out on an external network and a network utility tool is used to understand how the SSYN attack uses the vulnerability of the TCP three-way handshake.

In order to protect a server from application layer DoS and DDoS attacks, different available mitigation Web Application Firewalls such as Iptables, ModSecurity, and Mod Evasive are shown in the practical part. In addition, an explanation how a load balancer and other methods can be used in mitigating application layer and volumetric attacks is given from the technical point of view.

1 Introduction

1.1 Background

In human history, people have used different ways to protest in order to make their voices heard and to show their objection to a particular topic. Likewise, there is a long history of encrypting messages and intentions to intercept them by persons who are not the addressees: When looking back at ancient times, the powerful have always used mechanisms like lead and seal to make sure their letters would arrive unopened.

Today, we are in the age of technology which has made it easier for different parties to express their opinion by using social media, creating websites, and blogging. At the same time, some groups are trying to make their voices heard or just performing attacks because they can by taking down governments, private enterprises (online banking, gaming websites and services) or organizations. Nowadays, the amount of hacking attacks has reached a global level and it has become a threat to national security and the economy:

"When customer or internal services go down due to DDoS attacks, the impact is usually severe and affects the business in multiple ways. These include lost revenue and profit, lower productivity, higher costs due to penalties or breaches of service level agreement (SLA) contracts, and tarnished reputation or brand" [Arbor Networks 2011b, p. 2].

The intentions behind such attacks can be manifold. In the past years, hacking groups like Anonymous, Syrian Electronic Army and Lulzsec have caused the breakdown of entire systems, websites and online services of enterprises and organizations, to express their political views (calling themselves "hacktivists"), to make a general statement and to show the world that they are capable to do so.

According to Zach Capers, certified fraud examiner, the four major motivations for DDoS attacks are ideology, extortion, competition, and fraud [cf. Capers 2013]. In April 2014, the hacktivist group Anonymous performed a cyberattack on the Israeli government websites to remember the first anniversary of the attack they performed in April 2013 by taking down a number of Israeli websites, including those of the Defense Ministry and the Prime Minister's office. In their statement they explained

1

that they performed this attack in retaliation for "crimes against humanity" which the group says the Israeli government committed against Palestinians [cf. Fry 2014].

The usual architecture of the Internet is the following: There is a server on one end providing a specific service, for example a web server. This web server handles requests coming from the other end, in this case users who want to access data stored on that server. The number of requests or users of a server depends on the capacity of the hardware and how it is configured by the administrator. Different individuals, hacktivist groups or even governments try to attack theses servers, in order to damage the business or reputation of a company or organization. An attacker may use only one computer to connect to the server and send malicious packets, in order to malfunction the server and to make it unavailable for eligible users. In this case, when only one computer is used to perform the attack, it is called Denial of Service (DoS). When organized criminal groups compromise thousands, even up to millions of personal computers and try to send multiple gigabytes of data directed to the victim's server to perform the outrage of the service, this is called Distributed Denial of Service, DDoS.

How can so much traffic be generated? The traffic is generated by using botnets. Botnets are a collection of personal computers which are affected by malware. The most common way that a botnet master compromises a personal computer is using a common attack called phishing attack. The course of actions that takes place when a botnet master infects a system is: the user unintentionally installs a Trojan by opening an unknown email or visiting a malicious website. Then this Trojan opens a backdoor, which is used to install all the necessary tools and to establish a connection to the bot master. As a consequence, the affected computer becomes part of a big network, which is used to send malicious traffic to the targeted server.

In the following sub-chapter, overviews of existing categories of DDoS attacks are given.

1.2 Categories of DDoS attacks

The first DDoS attack started in 1989 from a single source with ICMP / Ping flood and nowadays DDoS attacks exceed 300 Gbps [cf. defense.net 2014]. One thing to notice in this time frame is how a DDoS attack has been increasing in size. Even if DDoS attacks are known for their big traffic there are still DDoS attacks executed single handedly or by using a laptop. Depending on the capacity of the DDoS source, the attack is differentiated in two categories: firstly, volumetric DDoS attacks that require a high bandwidth, and secondly, application layer attacks which are performed with less resources and a low bandwidth.

1.2.1 Volumetric DDoS attacks

This attack mainly uses the resources of other compromised systems to build up the big traffic which is necessary to perform the attacks. As a consequence, the success rate of the attack is mainly dependent on the amount of bandwidth or the number of bots the attacker uses to execute the attack:

"These attacks try to overwhelm the network infrastructure (e.g., routers, switches, etc.) with bandwidth-consuming assaults such as Internet Control Message Protocol (ICMP) or User Datagram Protocol (UDP) floods. Alternatively, they can attempt to overwhelm servers, load-balancers and firewalls by using Transmission Control Protocol (TCP) state exhaustion attacks such as TCP SYN floods and idle session attacks" [Arbor Networks 2011b, p.3].

Three of the most common volumetric DDoS attacks are TCP SYN Flooding, UDP Flooding, and HTTP GET flooding. The details are discussed below:

1.2.1.1 TCP SYN flooding attack:

This attack uses the vulnerability which exists in the implementation of the 3-way handshake that is used to start a TCP connection between a client and a server. When a client wants to establish a connection, the first step is to send SYN packet which contains the IP address of the client and other information to the server. In the second step, the server starts a new session, allocates the resource needed and replies to the client with SYN/ACK packet. In the last step, to conclude the handshake the client replies to the server with the ACK packet.

To execute this attack the attacker starts the processes of the 3-way handshake but never sends the ACK packet which is required to establish the connection. In this case, the server waits for the ACK packet with the assigned session and resource. The server will reallocate the resource after waiting for a specific time without getting the ACK packet. Yet, the attacker will execute this process in a mass volume of traffic and with a number of resources. When this repeats itself constantly, the server will not be able to function properly [cf. Janssen 2010-1014].

1.2.1.2 UDP flooding attack

UDP is another protocol, which does not need to perform a 3-way handshake, since it does not need to establish a connection:

"A UDP flood is a network flood and still one of the most common floods today. The attacker sends UDP packets, typically large ones, to single destination or to random ports. In most cases the attackers spoof the SRC IP which is easy to do since the UDP protocol is "connectionless" and does not have any type of handshake mechanism or session" [Radware 2013a].

1.2.1.3 Request-flooding attacks

In this category of attack, the attackers use a request GET URL, which is the same as the normal user's URL and which makes it more challenging to mitigate:

"An HTTP GET flood is a type of Layer 7 application attack that utilizes the standard valid GET requests used to fetch information, as in typical URL data retrievals (images, information, etc.) during SSL sessions. An HTTP GET flood is a volumetric attack that does not use malformed packets, spoofing or reflection techniques" [Les 2013].

1.2.2 Application-layer DDoS attacks

The application layer is the seventh layer in the Open Systems Interconnection (OSI). The main difference between the volumetric DDoS attack and the application layer DDoS attack is that the application layer DDoS attack has less volume of traffic and the attacker rather tries to exploit the application or to utilize the resource of the application by sending a systematically manipulated request:

"It consists of protocols that focus on process-to-process communication across an IP network and provides a firm communication interface and end-user services" [Janssen 2010-2014b].

4

Some of the protocols in the application layer are Hyper Text Transfer Protocol (HTTP), Simple Mail Transfer Protocol (SMTP), File Transfer protocol (FTP) and Domain Name System (DNS). These protocols are targeted by the attackers to perform the DDoS attack.

Below are some of the common application layer attacks:

1.2.2.1 Asymmetric workload attacks

This attack is common among attackers who have fewer resources and who want to perform DDoS attacks. A famous example that was reflected in the media was "the Jester (aka th3j35t3r)", a former US solder or "patriot hacker", who used an asymmetric attack to expose Anonymous, Wikileaks and other groups who he believed had done bad against the US government [cf. OConnor 2011, p.2]. The asymmetric attack can be explained in the following manner:

"Each attack session sends a higher proportion of requests that are more taxing on the server in terms of one or more specific resources. The request rate within a session is not necessarily higher than normal. This attack differs from the request-flooding attack in that it causes more damage per request by selectively sending heavier requests. Moreover, this attack can be invoked at a lower request rate, thereby requiring less work from the attacker and making detection increasingly difficult" [Ranjan et al. 2006, p.2].

1.2.2.2 Repeated one-shot attacks

As the name indicates, the attack is performed by manipulating a packet and causes the necessary damage on the targeted server, which in turn interrupts the normal service:

"This attack class is a degenerate case of the asymmetric workload attack, where the attacker sends only one heavy request in a session instead of sending multiple heavy requests per session. Thus, the attacker spreads its workload across multiple sessions instead of across multiple requests in a few sessions. The benefits of spreading are that the attacker is able to evade detection and potential service degradation to the session by closing it immediately after sending the request" [Ranjan et al. 2006, p.2].

5

1.2.2.3 Application-exploit attacks

Exploit attacks are common in different levels of software, in operating system levels of Microsoft Windows and different open source operating systems like Ubuntu. Different attackers try to find a weakness in the software or application and try to gain access and do more damage. As a consequence, the applications in this layer are vulnerable for the attackers to exploit. In this way of performing, a DDoS attack does not require big traffic, instead, the attackers need to pin out that vulnerability which can affect the application for the service and disrupt it from providing its normal usage: *"The attack vectors here are vulnerabilities in applications, for instance, hidden-field manipulation, buffer overflows, scripting vulnerabilities, cross-site scripting, cookie poisoning, and SQL injection"* [Kostadinov 2013].

1.3 Challenges for DDoS defense

The activities of hacktivists have not remained unnoticed. States have become aware of the challenges regarding the global issues of cyber, information and communication technology security and are trying to tackle these challenges through policies, strategies and laws. In 2011, the Obama Administration launched the U.S. International Strategy for Cyberspace, stating the following:

"Acknowledging that cybersecurity is a global issue that must be addressed with national efforts on the part of all countries, we will expand and regularize initiatives focused on cybersecurity capacity building – with enhanced focus on awareness-raising, legal and technical training, and support for policy development. Such programs must address more than purely technology issues; we will work with states to recognize the breadth of the cybersecurity challenge, assist them in developing their own strategies, and build capacity across the whole range of sectors – from network security and the establishment of Computer Emergency Readiness Teams (CERTs), to international law enforcement and defense collaboration, to productive relationships with the domestic and international private sector and civil society" [White House 2011, p.15].

Since 2012, the 57 participating States of the Organization for Security and Co-operation in Europe (OSCE), which is the largest regional security organization worldwide, decided to cooperate also in the area of cybersecurity [cf. Zannier 2014, p. 4]. In December 2013, all participating States agreed in a politically binding decision on an "initial set of OSCE confidence-building measures to reduce the risks of conflict stemming from the use of information and communication technologies" [OSCE 2013, p.1]. The voluntary measures include provisions for communication and information sharing at government and expert level, for creating a shared vocabulary related to security and use of ICTs, and for encouraging national legislation to facilitate co-operation on countering criminal or terrorist misuse of ICTs [cf. Zannier 2014, p. 5].

There is no doubt that the size of malicious traffic has increased considerably over the past decade. Even if states decide to work together, each government highly rely on experts to examine the challenges of attacks from a technical perspective.

The first step to minimize the large size of malicious traffic is to create awareness among users about malicious software, i.e. not to open suspicious emails, attachments and not to visit websites, which can make the personal computer vulnerable to be infected with Trojans. The next step would be to reduce the vulnerability of their system by installing anti-virus software to protect their personal computers and by keeping it up to date.

However, due to the remarkable increase of electronic devices in the last decade, i.e. the enlarged usage of personal computers, tablets and smart phones with internet connection, this has proven to become more and more difficult. The number of internet users has exploded over the last decade and also reached people who are not necessarily computer literate or experts. To explain these advanced levels of necessary security measures is a considerable challenge, costly and time-consuming. This means, one cannot rely on the responsibility of each user to minimize the volume of traffic, which is used for the attack. Therefore, measures have to be implemented by the internet service provider (ISP) or by the organization responsible for the service.

However, this is easier said than done because also ISPs and organizations find considerable challenges: Security hardware and software which are already in place for all networks such as firewalls and ISP devices cannot be used to protect a network or an application from a DDoS attack. The use of firewall is mainly to stop unauthorized Internet users from accessing a private network and the firewall

7

manages this by keeping track of all connections in a connection table. During a DDoS attack depending on the size of the attack, the firewall cannot create a connection for the arriving packets, making the firewall itself even a bottleneck [cf. Radware 2013b, p. 43]. Therefore, companies need to make large investments in new technologies, which are capable of mitigating and protecting the network from a DDoS attack.

As in most of the cases, the hackers' initiatives have aimed at destroying a system or at gaining access, for administrators it is challenging to protect their system since they do not know which part of their system an attacker is trying to exploit and how they are performing the attack. In addition, attackers have no time constraints and can try again and again when they fail in their attempts.

According to the American Arbor Networks Corporation, "(...), today may be the most challenging time ever faced by data center operators and security teams" [Arbor Networks 2011a, p. 4], because:

"1. Attacks are getting larger (i.e., volumetric attacks are getting bigger).

2. Attacks are getting more sophisticated (i.e., new application-layer attacks or combined volumetric and application-layer attacks are becoming more common).

3. Data center attacks are getting more frequent (i.e., multi-tenant, Internet-facing data centers are becoming the new prime targets for attackers)" [Arbor Networks 2011a, p. 4].

1.4 State-of-the-art of DDoS defense

Currently, according to Incapsula's (an American IT security company) research team, DDoS attacks in 2014 are becoming smarter, bigger, faster and stronger [cf. Shatz 2014], which makes it challenging for potential victims of an attack to update their system constantly and to implement a more efficient system in place which can mitigate these attacks more effectively. Attacks are constantly taking place on the Internet putting China and the US as the main sources of DDoS attacks [cf. Digitalattackmap.com]. Small and medium businesses providing their services and selling their products using the Internet, have becoming under threat by DDoS attacks. In the first place, they do not have mitigation systems in place, so they see themselves forced to pay an external private security company to handle and mitigate these attacks.

1.5 Contribution of the Thesis

This master thesis concentrates on the different DDoS attacks available nowadays and determines how a network and a system can be protected from these attacks. The paper contains two main parts: the first one is the theoretical part, which covers a detailed description of different DDoS attacks, the effects an attack has on an enterprise, as well as touch upon the current status-quo of research literature and latest discussions within the scientific community.

The second part is the practical part, which shows in detail the DDoS attack on the Layer 3 (Network Layer) and Layer 4 (Transport Layer) targeting the network infrastructure. By demonstrating these attacks, it shows in particular the UDP reflection and amplification attacks. In addition, it tries to show what effects it has on the Layer 7 (application layer) and on DDoS attacks targeting the application layer. Finally, it looks at the existing mechanisms and configurations to mitigate the DDoS attack and to keep a system up and running for the required time.

Media reports in the news related to companies being attacked by a DDoS are more and more frequent. With online tutorials and tools to perform attacks, it has become easy to perform these attacks even without having detailed technical knowledge. The main question therefore is, if it is possible to completely mitigate DDoS attacks on the different layers and which ways of mitigation methods can be effective by looking at different models currently available.

1.6 Chapter outline

In this part the highlight of each chapter is presented to give the impression of the contents of each chapter.

Chapter 2: there are many tools on the internet for free used to perform a DoS attack. This chapter will look in detail at the tools used by the different groups mainly to carry out a DoS attack from a single client. The tool that will be discussed mainly

9

is the Low Orbit Ion Canon (LOIC), how the attack from the tool affects the server, the difference between a fake traffic generated by the LOIC tool and a traffic generated by genuine host will be analyzed by using a network utility tool.

Chapter 3: presents the DDoS attacks which are performed by a high bandwidth of traffic, mainly targeting the network layer and Transport layer. The tool MeTuS Delphi will be discussed in detail: the steps needed before setting up the tool, how the virus on the tool can be created, how the hosts can be infected and at last demonstrates how a volumetric attack can be carried out by using the hosts compromised.

Chapter 4: After demonstrating the attacks on application layer, network layer and transport layer in the previous two chapters. This chapter will demonstrate how a network administrator can protect a system and how he can mitigate attacks. The different techniques available and recommended will be discussed. In addition a practical mitigation implementation of an attack by setting up tools used to mitigate the attacks before affecting the server.

Chapter 5: concludes the thesis by summarizing the research contributions, the challenges faced during the researching on the different topics, what best practices can be recommended in protecting a system from denial of service attacks and at last by proposing possible directions for future research.

2 Practical Application of DoS

Up to now the previous parts have been discussing the background of DoS and DDoS attack, the different categories and the current status of the art has been discussed in detail. In this chapter, the thesis will try to implement a simulation of a real world scenario by using available resources and a virtualization software.

Performing scientific experiments related to practical applications of DoS (Denial of Service) or DDoS (Distributed Denial of Service) attacks in the real world is a challenging task. If caught trying to attack an existing company's webserver, the attacker could run the risk of being charged with a criminal offence unless it is supported by a company to test the strengths and weaknesses of its own security measures against DoS attacks through a planned application. In practice, companies commission IT experts to apply a virtual attack on their webserver with the aim of testing how long it takes to take down their online service and, as a consequence, putting counter measures in place based on the results from the test. In this case, a specific time schedule has to be agreed in order not to interfere with the experts' test. In addition, it is important to send out a notification to all users, i.e. employees and customers, who could be accessing in the time frame in which the test takes place.

Therefore, for the scientific purposes of the underlying thesis, an artificial webserver had to be created by using a personal computer, in addition to a laptop depending on the different attacks needed to demonstrate. As there are not enough machines to install all the important operating systems needed to create the scenarios with an attacker, regular users and the victim's server, an Oracle VM VirtualBox was used to install the different operating systems. The required tools were installed on the one side on the operating system to attack the server, and on the other side on the operating system which was used as server, depending on the type of service the system is providing.

In the following paragraph, the specific set up of the network will be described in more detail and the task of each machine highlighted.

2.1 Set up of the network of three machines

On the VirtualBox, a network of three separate machines was set up, all of them running an Ubuntu 14.04 operating system.

The first machine was set up with an Apache server hosting a website to be accessed from different networks. After setting up the Apache 2 server, it was possible to check the status of the server, in order to see the maximum number of connections the Apache 2 server can support. These connections are shown in various ways symbolically represented in Figure 1 below, which is a part of a screenshot taken from the status of the Apache server:

PID	Connections		Threads		Async connections		
	total	accepting	busy	idle	writing	keep-alive	closing
2863	0	yes	0	25	0	0	0
2864	0	yes	1	24	0	0	0
Sum	0		1	49	0	0	0

1 requests currently being processed, 49 idle workers

Figure 29: Normal Apache status

The figure shows the general status of the Apache server, i.e. how many connections the server can handle at one time, the number of requests it is handling at the specific time, and the number of idle workers, which are ready to take a request. At the time the screenshot was taken, only one request was processed, while 49 workers were idle. This request was from the server itself checking the status. Each process ID ("PID") has 25 threads, so the more processes are added for the server to handle, the more requests it can handle. The Async connection specifies the number of requests are currently writing (meaning sending requests), keeping-alive (meaning the number of connections that have to be maintained between the server and the client), and closing (meaning the number of connections that are about to be terminated).

The first symbol represented by a line ("-") means *"waiting for connection"*. The second symbol represented by dot (".") means *"open slot with no current process"*. For each request sent from a client to a server one thread is assigned to the specific request for the time until the client decides to disconnect from the server. When a thread is assigned to a specific request on the Apache status window, the "Waiting for connection" is changing to "Starting up" ("S"), "Reading request" ("R"), or "Sending reply" ("W") and when disconnecting, the symbol changes to "Closing connection" ("C"). This is how all the available threads are used by the Apache 2 server and how the server handles each request within a reasonable replying time.

The second machine is the attacker, which is running the Ubuntu 14.04 operating system, and it is installed with the tool Low Orbit Ion Cannon (LOIC) version 1.1.1.26. The LOIC is originally a tool for Microsoft Windows, so for running LOIC, it is necessary to pre-install the software monodevelop, mono-gmcs, mono-mcs and liblog4net-cil-dev, so that LOIC can be compiled and built on the Ubuntu machine. A detailed description of LOIC, including how it is working, will be discussed in the coming sub-chapter.

The third virtual machine is again an Ubuntu 10.04 operating system. It is possible to use any other operating system since it will be used only to access the service provided by the Apache 2 server.

The next step after setting up the network is accessing a website from an outside host.

2.2 Accessing a website from an outside host

The Apache server is configured to listen to all requests sent to port 80 and to its specific address. The Ubuntu host establishes a connection with the server and sends an HTTP request using the domain name or the IP address of the server on a browser. Figure 2 is a screenshot from the packet sniffed by the network tool Wireshark during the communication of the server and the client.

It shows the list of the request header fields with the appropriate parameters. One of the important request header field is the *"Host"* that specifies the host, which is sending the request, and the port number of the service it is requesting.

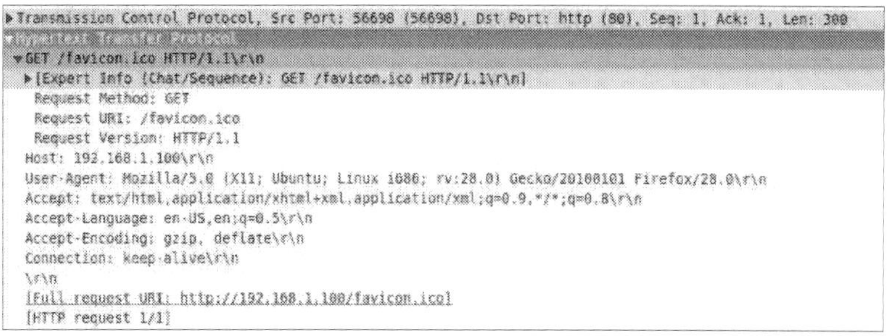

▶ Transmission Control Protocol, Src Port: 56698 (56698), Dst Port: http (80), Seq: 1, Ack: 1, Len: 300
▼ Hypertext Transfer Protocol
▼ GET /favicon.ico HTTP/1.1\r\n
  ▶ [Expert Info (Chat/Sequence): GET /favicon.ico HTTP/1.1\r\n]
    Request Method: GET
    Request URI: /favicon.ico
    Request Version: HTTP/1.1
  Host: 192.168.1.100\r\n
  User-Agent: Mozilla/5.0 (X11; Ubuntu; Linux i686; rv:28.0) Gecko/20100101 Firefox/28.0\r\n
  Accept: text/html,application/xhtml+xml,application/xml;q=0.9,*/*;q=0.8\r\n
  Accept-Language: en-US,en;q=0.5\r\n
  Accept-Encoding: gzip, deflate\r\n
  Connection: keep-alive\r\n
  \r\n
  [Full request URI: http://192.168.1.100/favicon.ico]
  [HTTP request 1/1]

Figure 30: Normal HTTP request from a genuine client

The practical application showed that while accessing the service provided by the webserver, the time it took to respond and show the requested website was approximately less than 500ms

In the following paragraph, a description of the attacking tools used during this practical application, i.e. LOIC and HTTP DoS, will be given.

2.3 Attacking tools: LOIC and HTTP DoS tools

LOIC stands for Low Orbit Ion Cannon and was originally developed by Praetox Technologies as a stress testing application [cf. Pras/ Sperotto/ Moura et al. 2010, p. 2] written in C#. Afterwards, LOIC became available within the public domain, in which it started to be used for DoS and DoS attacks. Figure 3 below shows a LOIC interface with www.google.com IP address taken as an example:

14

Figure 31: LOIC tool interface

On the LOIC interface the features are categorized mainly into three parts: The first part being "Select your target" where the attacker can enter the Uniform Resource Locator (URL) or the IP address of the server to be attacked (in this case www.google.com). Next to both text boxes are the "Lock on" buttons, which check the server and display the IP address of the server. When the attacker has entered the web address of the victim's server, the specific IP address is shown on the selected target. The second part is the "Attack options", with the "Port" being one of the important options: if the correct port is not specified, the attack might not achieve the goal successfully. Next to the "Port" is the "Method", which gives the three attack options: TCP, UDP and HTTP in the drop box. As discussed in the first chapter, depending on which method we choose, it decides on which layer the DoS attack will be committed. The next part used to control the intensity of the attack is the "Speed" sliding bar. Sliding the bar to the left increases the speed of the traffic sent to the server, and sliding it to the opposite, decreases the speed gradually. The third part corresponds to "Ready?", which has a button "IMMA CHARGIN MAH LAZER". The button is used to start the attack after all the settings discussed above on the LOIC are set to the right configuration.

As it can be seen in the above discussion of the LOIC, it is easy to use by using few steps in a user friendly graphic interface and it achieves its goal by taking down services effectively. However, one disadvantage of using LOIC is that it is not possible to hide the IP address of the attacker as we can see in the Wireshark

15

sniffed packets or even by opening the Apache Server status: here, the attacker's real IP address appears in the list without using any additional technique or tool. To achieve anonymity, it is necessary to use Tor or any other tool, which are used to spoof IP addresses.

2.4 Practical application: creation of an attack scenario

For the purpose of the underlying thesis, a practical attack scenario was created, in order to demonstrate how the attack affects the webserver and differences that can be noticed between the normal user traffic and the attacking traffic. In the following paragraphs, a detailed description of the respective steps will be given.

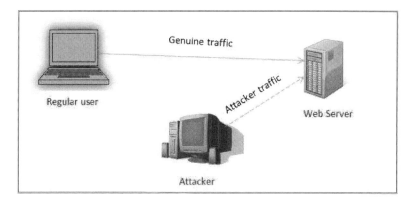

Figure 32: Network diagram of DoS attack

As described above, for this scenario of an attack three parties were used: (i) the webserver, (ii) a normal user, who is trying to access the web page provided by the web server, and the last one is (iii) the attacker, who tries to disrupt the normal function of the web server.

First, the normal user tries to access the web page by entering the IP address of the server. Observation in the practical application showed that the response of the server was ~500ms and all the content of the web page was displayed without any delay.

The attacker was equipped with the tools used to perform DoS attacks: LOIC and Slowloris http dos. In addition, the attacker had the IP address of the server which

16

he targetcd to flood. By entering the IP address in the text box of the LOIC and pressing the button "Lock on", the IP address was successfully shown on "Selected target" that gave a confirmation that the target was reachable.

As a next step, in the second part of the LOIC tool the port number was set up. In this case the port number was set to 80. In this scenario the target was to execute a DoS attack on the Application layer level, therefore, the method was set to "HTTP". At first, the speed of the attack was set at a slower rate and it was increased every 30 seconds at a constant rate. This served to analyze at which speed the response of the server time started to be affected.

After the attack was started at a slower rate, it showed that the response speed of the server was affected. The normal client had to wait between two and three seconds to get a response from the server side. As the speed of the attack increased steadily, the server stopped responding to the requests from the genuine user and also the Apache server was not responding to the request from the local host (Server) for the current status.

Attack status						
Idle	Connecting	Requesting	Downloading	Downloaded	Requested	Failed
0	0	0	10	297	307	0

Figure 33: LOIC attack status toolbar

Figure 5 shows the status of the LOIC attack: the "Requested" column shows the number of requests sent within the limited amount of time after the attack started. The "Downloaded" shows the successful responded requests from the server.

17

111 requests currently being processed, 39 idle workers

PID	Connections		Threads		Async connections		
	total	accepting	busy	idle	writing	keep-alive	closing
3094	21	yes	25	0	0	0	0
4485	0	yes	25	0	0	0	0
4313	18	yes	25	0	0	0	0
4341	11	yes	25	0	0	0	0
4513	10	yes	10	15	0	0	0
4541	0	yes	1	24	0	0	0
Sum	60		111	39	0	0	0

RRRRRRRRRRRRRRRRRRRRRRRRRRRRRRRRRRRRRRRRRRRRRRRRRRRRRRRRRRRRRRRRRRRR
RRRRRRRRRRRRRRRRRRRRRRRRRRRRRRRRRRRRRRRRR____RRRRRRRRRR_____
____W_____

Figure 34: Status of Apache server under attack

While the server was under a full speed attack it was not possible to check the status of the Apache server from the local host, so this screenshot was taken while the LOIC tool speed was set at a lower rate. Compared to Figure 1 of the normal Apache server status that has only two processes (each of them handling 25 requests), the Figure 6, taken during the attack, has six processes (again each of them handling 25 requests). From the result of the attack, we can understand that the Apache server was forced to create more processes as the existing threads started to become busy by handling requests from different clients.

As the LOIC tool flooded the server with http requests, the Apache server continued assigning the available threads for the incoming requests. At the same time, the server continued doing likewise until it ran out of resources to create more processes.

In general, threads drop a connection or a request from a client when the connection already established reaches a timeout. The timeout for a connection is specified in the configuration file of the Apache server. Once the timeout is reached, the thread will be available again to be assigned to a task by the server. However, as long as the DoS attack is not stopped, the threads will be assigned again to the same kind of connection.

In the paragraph below, the consequences it has on the webserver when being attacked by DoS and how it comes to the point of crashing down, will be explained.

2.5 Effects shown when attacked by DoS

The server came to a state of outrage, when the resource of the server became exhausted and could not handle requests anymore. It was not also handling requests coming from a genuine client. Even if the attack from the LOIC tool was stopped, the server was still not responsive until the three minutes timeout of the Apache server for a connection was ended. After the time out of a connection, threads were free and ready to accept a new request from another host.

As mention in the above paragraph during the attack the resources of the server which is hosting the webserver are affected directly and that affects the functionality of the online service. Therefore, to see the utilization of the resources, during the period of the attack on the Apache server, a Glances system monitoring tool was running in the background to analyze which resources are affected by the attack. Figure 7 was a screenshot taken from the tool during the attack.

CPU	96.5%	nice:	0.0%	LOAD	1-core	MEM	60.8%	SWAP	5.0%
user:	75.6%	irq:	0.0%	1 min:	1.24	total:	1002M	total:	1022M
system:	20.6%	iowait:	0.0%	5 min:	0.89	used:	610M	used:	51.4M
idle:	3.5%	steal:	0.0%	15 min:	0.58	free:	392M	free:	971M

Figure 35: Glance resource monitoring results during attack

The Ubuntu Glance system monitoring tool uses four different colors on the values of the resources to indicate the level of risk on the usage. In Figure 7, three of the colors can be seen, "Green" representing the usage of the of the resource is normal, "Blue" gives a sign that the resource usage is above the normal, "Violet" is to alert that the resource over used and "Red" is shown in critical case when the resource is near to be fully utilized.

Before that attack on the server started, the percentage of the CPU usage on the "user" side was 7.3% and "system" usage was 2.1%, taking the total percentage to 9.4%. The remaining 90.6% was idle. However, with in the first six seconds after the attack from the LOIC client started, the percentage of the "user" jumped to 75.6% and the "system" increased to 20.6%. The memory showed also change, before the attack the used memory was 372M, after the attack started the memory consumption increased to 610M, causing also the change of the color code from "Green" to "Blue" indicating the stiff increase of usage of the memory.

From this it can be seen the first resource fully utilized by the Apache server was the CPU, the color code "Violet" on the 75.6% of the "user" is also alerting the administrator on the usage of the resource. Increasing the capacity of the CPU will help the Apache server to handle more requests or when it is under attack, to endure longer. However, this does not mean CPU is the only resource that needs upgrading. The memory has also shown usage difference after the attack started. Therefore, even if the CPU has more power, the next resource to be affect by the attack will be the memory.

The Glance tool also logs, giving a warning and when the usage of the resources gets to a critical point. Figure 8 shows the last five logs made by the tool at different periods of the attack. All the logs were made only on the "CPU_USER".

```
Warning or critical alerts (lasts 5 entries)
2014-09-10 04:20:17 (0:02:21) - WARNING on CPU_USER
2014-09-10 04:17:48 (0:01:20) - WARNING on CPU_USER
2014-09-10 04:16:07 (0:00:03) - CRITICAL on CPU_USER (94.0)
2014-09-10 03:53:26 (0:00:13) - CRITICAL on CPU_USER
2014-09-10 03:48:02 (0:01:01) - WARNING on CPU_USER
```

Figure 36: Glance warning and alerts log

In this part, the exhaustion of the resources during the attack and from this, it is possible to conclude that the upgrading of the resources cannot be a solution to protect the server from DDoS attack. A server can be running on a server with a high resource quota. However, the high resource specification does not mean the server is protected from the DDoS attack. The only difference can be that the time for the attackers to take down the server will be longer or the number of botnets they have should be bigger.

2.6 Difference on request sent

Different DoS attack tools succeed in executing attacks by sending a considerable size of traffic in high speed. In case of an HTTP flooding attack, the HTTP request packets are generated randomly. In general, these kinds of packets have similar characteristics, such as the same name, the same size or the same time created. Below is the screenshot of the packet sniffed by using the Wireshark tool during the attack from the LOIC tool:

```
▼ Hypertext Transfer Protocol
  ▶ GET / HTTP/1.1\n
    Accept: */*\n
    User-Agent: Mozilla/4.0 (compatible; MSIE 7.0; Windows NT 6.0)\n
    Accept-Encoding: gzip, deflate\n
    Host: 192.168.1.100\n
    \n
    [Full request URI: http://192.168.1.100/]
    [HTTP request 1/1]
    [Response in frame: 631]
```

Figure 37: HTTP request sent from LOIC tool

In Figure 9 it shows the packet detail of the HTTP request sent from the LOIC client. The packet detail is smaller than normal HTTP request sent from a client shown in Figure 2. The LOIC HTTP request is missing most of the HTTP request header fields like: "Accept" which is used to define the media types which are acceptable for the response, Accept-Language is used to restrict the languages which can be used in the response of the request and Connection is a field used to specify weather that specific connection should be kept alive or closed. From this it can be observed that the LOIC tool is using a normal packet without details by just covering up the packet as an HTTP request.

This specific difference can be pointed out easily and is used as one condition in some Intrusion Detection Systems (IDS) like Snort. By using this condition in the rules of the tool used to protect the server or to alert the network administrator that the system is under attack.

21

3 Practical Application of DDoS

In the previous chapters, we have seen the tools and the ways how we can execute denial of service attacks from a single host. The attack from the single host was enough to disrupt the service the webserver was providing. The effect of the attack on the server was shown within a few seconds after the tool started the flooding by sending the bad traffic. The webserver did not manage to handle the fake requests sent from the tool because the server resource was limited to handling only small amounts of traffic.

Big companies and organizations have servers with a high performance capability; the online services provided by banks, insurance companies and private enterprises such as Amazon, eBay and many other, are accessed by thousands or even millions of users at the same time. These servers can handle all the traffic without any problem. Famous large-scale attacks, which were executed by different hacktivists on the worldwide known corporations Amazon, PayPal, BankAmerica, PostFinance, MasterCard and Visa, would not have been possible by using a single attacking host. Therefore, these hacktivist groups were using advanced tools, which helped them perform these large-scale attacks. Before starting this kind of attacks they used different tools and techniques to compromise thousands of hosts in different geographical locations all over the world without the knowledge of the host owner. These sets of compromised hosts are known as "botnets". Then by using the resources of all compromised hosts the attacker – in this case the botnet master –, can perform attacks on the online service of the targeted company.

Below, the DDoS attacking tools is discussed in detail, namely, how the tools are used to create and manage the botnet. In addition, it will be shown how the attacks are organized by these tools to bring down the targeted online service of a company or an organization.

3.1 DDoS attacking tool

As mentioned above, different hacktivist groups have been using different tools. Some hacktivists program the tools themselves, while others use tools which are already available online to create the botnet and to commit the attack. Such an example for an already available online tool is the MeTuS Delphi 2.8 tool: MeTuS

Delphi 2.8 is one of the common tools used by different groups of users, from people who want to build a private botnet up to organized criminals.

Downloading and finding the necessary documents was challenging: In general, both, the tools and their respective documentations which are used by different hacktivist groups, are hard to find online, since the websites providing these resources will be blocked by the company hosting the website or by a government watch dog, which is responsible for cyber security. In addition, when finding a website providing the resources, the links are leading to advertisements instead of directing to the downloading window. Therefore, most of them are scams. For this research, it was possible to download a "safe" copy of the MeTuS Delphi 2.8; however, the amount spent for investigating the right source was considerable.

3.2 MeTuS Delphi 2.8

When downloading the MeTuS Delphi 2.8, there are four files included:

> ➤ ca_setup - is Cain & Able which is a password recovery tool for Microsoft operating systems. It allows easy recovery of several kinds of passwords by sniffing the network, cracking encrypted passwords using dictionary, brute-force and cryptanalysis attacks, recording VoIP conversations, decoding scrambled passwords, recovering wireless network keys, revealing password boxes, uncovering cached passwords and analyzing routing protocols [cf. Oxid.it 2009].

> ➤ ducsetup – is a dynamic DNS update client, which continually checks for IP address changes in the background and automatically updates the DNS at No-IP whenever it changes [cf. noip.com 2014]. It is also possible to download this application from the no-ip website when creating a host which is bounded to the IP address of the computer. How this tool will be used is described in the next part.

> ➤ MeTuS Delphi 2.8 – is the executable for the MeTuS Delphi application, which is used to build the virus named "Server" that will infect the victim's computer.

- ➢ stub – is a file created by a crypter to keep a program encrypted and undetectable by anti-virus software. The stub is needed to create the virus, which will be used to infect the computers.

When unzipping the WinRAR file, which contained all the above files, the anti-virus tool was deleting some of the files detecting them as a virus. Therefore, it was needed to deactivate the anti-virus during the implementation of this practical part. Another option to protect these files from being deleted by the anti-virus on the computer is to allow the specific files to be ignored by the anti-virus. This, of course, depends on the type of anti-virus installed on the computer.

The next part will explain the detailed setups needed to build the virus, which is used to infect the computers, and to make them part of the botnet.

3.3 Setting up the MeTuS Delphi tool

To use the MeTuS Delphi tool, there are two main prerequisite steps to follow. These are creating a no-ip host and port forwarding. They are mandatory, if the attacker is targeting to compromise hosts all over the world where there is internet. These two steps and in addition setting up the MeTuS Delphi tool will be discussed in detail in the following paragraphs.

3.3.1 Creating a no-ip host

In this case, for creating a botnet, the port forwarding is required so that when a client double clicks the virus built by using the MeTus Delphi tool, the virus creates a backdoor and tries to connect to the botmaster. Nevertheless, the computer of the botmaster needs to be accessible, even if it is behind a router.

One of the necessary things to setup, before starting to configure the MeTus Delphi tool, is to create a host, which is bound to the IP address of the computer of the botmaster. This serves to avoid the dynamic changing of the IP address of the router of the botmaster.

This problem of the dynamic changing can be solved by creating a host name on the www.no-ip.com. However, the website requires registration of the user to create a host name. When picking a name for the host, it is important that the name contains a maximum of four letters and it can only contain a combination of letters of the alphabet and numbers. It is also important to select the "no-ip.info" from all the domain names provided by the drop box of the no-ip host.

Creating the no-ip address with the host name is necessary, when the IP address of the botmaster is not static. The computer of the botmaster has to be configured by using the dynamic domain name system (DNS) updater. Otherwise, when the virus "server" is executed on the victim's computer, it cannot establish a connection with the computer of the botmaster after creating a backdoor.

From the same website, it is possible to download the "ducsetup" application, or in this case, it is provided in the downloaded MeTus Delphi folder. By using the application, it can be installed on the computer of the botmaster. When running the installed "ducsetup" it requires login by using the details that were used to register on the no-ip website when creating the host name. After that, the application is running in the background. It monitors any change of the IP address of the host and bind it to the host name created automatically, whenever the IP address is changed.

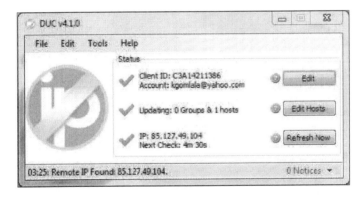

Figure 38: Dynamic DNS Update Client running in the background

The Figure 10 shows the screenshot of the DUC client running in the background ensuring the host is accessible from the outside network.

3.3.2 Port forwarding

According to the official website, "Port forwarding is a method of making a computer on your network accessible to computers on the Internet, even though you are

25

behind a router. It is commonly used for hosting game servers, peer to peer downloading, and voice over IP type applications. There are many other reasons you may need to forward a port, this is not an exhaustive list" [PortForward 2014].

The PortForward website mainly contains a guide on how to forward a port for most routers, which are available in different places to connect to the Internet. In this case, the private router which is used for this experiment is "FRITZBox Fon WLAN 7140 SL". It is important to get the port number, which is applied in the MeTus Delphi tool while building the virus "server". Otherwise, if the wrong port is used in the port forward configuration, the compromised hosts will not connect to the botnet master and therefore, they will not show up in the list of compromised hosts.

Figure 11 shows the setting of the FRITZBox router. "Port" 3174 is forwarded and under "an IP address" it shows the IP address of the local host.

		Liste der Portfreigaben				
Aktiv	Bezeichnung	Protokoll	Port	an IP-Adresse	an Port	
☑	BOT-Port	TCP	3174	192.168.178.23	3174	✎ ✕
					Neue Portfreigabe	

Figure 39: Router port forwarding setting

The PortForward website also provides a PortForward Network Utility called PFPortChecker. This tool helps to check whether the specific port or the range of ports forwarded on the router are open or not.

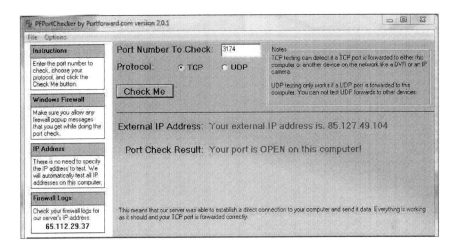

Figure 40: Result of the port forwarded on PFPortChecker

As it can be seen in Figure 12, the port "3174" is open. In addition, the network utility tool shows the external IP address connected to the port. Therefore, the tool also makes it possible to see that the dynamic DNS update client (DUC) is running in the background.

After successfully running the PFPortChecker utility tool and checking the two steps, i.e. creating a no-ip host and forwarding a specific port on the router, it is now possible to run the MeTus Delphi application and to proceed to the next step of creating the botnet.

3.3.3 Creating the Initialization File

The MeTus Delphi requires an initialization ".INI" file to save the configuration of the tool. The ".INI" file contains two parts, the section or name and the property. To create the ".INI" file, it requires filling some settings in the "Option" tab of the MeTus Delphi tool. The contents of the "Option" tab can be seen in Figure 13.

Figure 41: MeTus Delphi tool option tab

Before saving the settings of the tool, the main setting to enter is the "Auto-Listen Port". In this text box, the same port number which opened in part 3.3.3, Port forwarding step needs to be entered. The "Server Password" is required if the attacker needs to set a password for the tool. All the other settings are optional. After filling the required fields, pressing the "Save Settings" creates a file called "settings.ini" in the same folder where the MeTus Delphi tool is saved. All the configurations set in the "Options" tab can be seen in the ".INI" file. Figure 14 shows the screenshot of the "settings.ini" file.

```
1    [Settings]
2    Listen=3174
3    Password=
4    StubVer=2.84
5    Color=clBlack
6
```

Figure 42: The initialization file of the MeTus Delphi tool

3.3.4 Creating the "server" virus

To create the virus "server", it is required to use one of the executable applications downloaded called "MeTus Delphi 2.8" which can be seen in Figure 15.

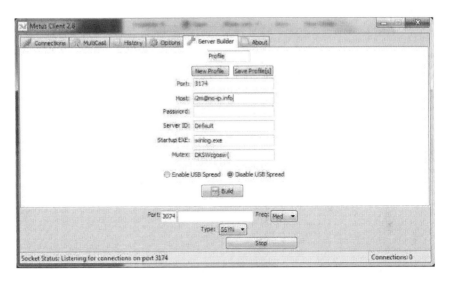

Figure 43: MeTus Delphi 2.8 tool server builder interface

As can be seen, there are some fields to fill which are specific to the host which is setting up the MeTus Delphi client. The first one is the "Port", in this case "3174". The same port number was used in the Port forwarding process of the router. The next text box "Host" is where the host name created on the www.no-ip.com with the domain name "no-ip.info" is entered. In this case, the host name created is "i2m@no-ip.info".

In the "host" part it is also possible to enter the IP address of the local host. Yet, the MeTus Delphi tool will be active in listening to connections from the open port until the computer is restarted or until the next time the dynamic IP address of the client is changed.

All the other texts were left as their default value as they were set by the client. Below the text boxes there are two option boxes: "Enable USB spread" and "Disable USB spread". The first option "Enable USB spread" should be selected, if the attacker is planning to spread the virus by directly plugging an infected USB stick on the computer of the victim. At the bottom of the client setting is the "Build" button, which will create the "server" virus in the folder where MeTus Delphi is located.

29

3.3.5 Infecting users

After setting up all the requirements on the MeTus Delphi client side and after building the "server" virus, the next step will be infecting user machines to increase the number of bots, which can be controlled by the botmaster. The botmaster can use different techniques. One way is by choosing the option "Enable USB spread" when building the virus. Spreading the virus by using a USB drive comes handy when the attacker has direct access to the host that he is targeting to infect. This method of distributing the virus makes public places providing free Internet on their computer vulnerable. Therefore, companies which are allowing their computers for public use need to take more caution. They should put strong security measures in place and keep their antivirus tools up to date in order to avoid becoming part of a botnet.

On the other hand, there are many ways to infect hosts when the attacker does not have direct access to the computer of the victim. One way of infecting a computer was noticed while doing research on the different techniques and tools used to create a botnet and carrying out a DDoS attack. There are many tutorials and YouTube videos explaining the steps needed to create a botnet, most of them even providing a link during the tutorial directing to where the tools can be downloaded. However, when downloading the MeTus Delphi tool, it already contains the "Server" virus in the folder and as discussed in part 3.3.4, the server is built by using a specific open port number and the IP address directing to an already existing botmaster. As persons with different levels of knowledge use these tutorials, they might execute the downloaded virus "Server" assuming it is the virus they created themselves during setting up the MeTus Delphi tool. This knowledge gap is used intentionally to deceive the users and to distribute the virus, as the experience of this practical implementation for the underlying thesis showed.

Therefore, this way of distributing the virus can be effective. Other ways to distribute the virus can be by sending out emails with the virus attachment to random contacts, or by binding a media file with the virus and uploading it to pirate sites or FTP sites. The most common method, however, which is used in social networks or chat rooms, is "social engineering". "Social engineering" refers to tricking Internet users to install malicious software while appearing friendly and social.

3.3.6 Compromised clients

After all the above steps are made, the next part is to wait for infected hosts to show up on the MeTus Delphi tool.

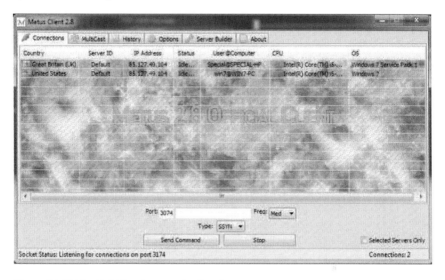

Figure 44: MeTus Delphi tool connection interface

In Figure 16, at the bottom of the bar, the "Socket Status" shows the status of the MeTus Delphi tool. Before the setting of the port forward and the DUC configuration, the status of the tool was "Closed". After setting up all the configurations needed for the tool to start listening, the status was changed to "Listening for connection on port 3174". This status change to listening can be taken as a confirmation that the configuration of the tool is successful and that a host executing the "Server" virus will appear in the list of compromised hosts. By right clicking on a client from the clients listed in the connection it is possible to "uninstall" that specific client, i.e. removing it from the list from the botnet, and to send a command "firefox" in order to get the passwords saved on the Mozilla Firefox browser.

The table in Figure 16 shows where the list of compromised hosts appears, when selecting the "Connection" tab. Some of the important fields in the "Connection" table are the following: the first field "Country" shows in which country the compromised hosts are located geographically. Yet, it does not always show the correct location. As we can see in the table above, the two compromised hosts are from United Kingdom and United States which is not correct, as the two hosts are in Austria. Therefore, the tool is not getting the country from the IP address or by using other techniques, but rather from the "Region and Language" setting in the control panel of the computer. Then, the second field in the table is "IP Address" where the IP address of the hosts is listed. "Status" is the third important field showing whether the specific host is online and available for the disposal of the botmaster. The last two fields are the "CPU" that helps to understand the resource of the host, and the "OS", showing which operating system is installed on the specific host.

3.4 DDoS attack using compromised hosts

The MeTus Delphi tool is mainly used to create a botnet, but once a host appears in the tools "Connection" table, the attacker can perform many other actions without the awareness of the owner of the computer. According to the Spy Emergency website, MeTus Delphi *"is (...) used to break into user system and grant access to the user data or perform malicious actions"* [SpyEmergency 2011, n.p.]. As the main interest of this research are DDoS attacks, in the next part the two possible ways of using MeTus Delphi to carry out a DDoS attack, will be focused on.

In Figure 16 of the MeTus Delphi tool "Connection" interface, in the lower part of the tool "Type" dropbox, there are two options of DDoS attacks: Slave Synchronisation ("SSYN") and "UDP". Both these attacks are on network layer and volumetric attacks. Therefore, the numbers of connections available on the botnet directly affect the success rate of the DDoS attack.

The first option "SSYN" was discussed in the first chapter of part 1.2.1.1. The "SSYN" uses the vulnerability of the TCP three-way handshake. MeTuS Delphi uses all connections available to send a "SYN" packet requesting a connection from the server. This attack exhausts the resources of the server by occupying a connection without sending the ACK packet and holding the assigned thread until the timeout of the thread is over.

The second option of the dropbox is the "UDP" flooding; UDP is a connectionless protocol, making it different from TCP. This attack sends a large number of UDP packets to different ports on the server, and the server checks if any application is running on the specific ports. Then, the server replies with an ICMP "Destination host unreachable" message after having verified that no application is running on the port. This way of handling the attack from the server side consumes the available resources and this inevitably leads to either the malfunction of the server or the server not managing to accept requests anymore.

3.4.1 Analyzing the attack from the MeTus Delphi tool

In Chapter two, it was shown how much an attack from a single client can affect the service of a webserver. An attack carried out by using a botnet can be more dangerous for even bigger systems capable of handling large traffic volumes. What makes the attack from the MeTus Delphi more harmful is that the attack is directed from all the machines compromised by the botnet master. Therefore, this makes it more difficult to identify a specific host responsible for the attack, since all the compromised hosts are attacking at the same time using their own IP address when flooding the server of the victim.

3.4.2 TCP/SSYN attack

Using the compromised hosts, a TCP attack was experimented by using the attack type "SSYN" on the MeTus Delphi tool. To understand the attack, a Wireshark network protocol analyzer was installed on the attacker's computer. At first, in order to understand how the TCP three-way handshake works, a normal request was made and the communication between the client and the server was recorded on the Wireshark tool, as can be seen in Figure 17.

32 39.559919886	10.8.2.15	93.184.221.39	TCP	74 40147 > http [SYN] Seq=0 Win=29200 Len=0 MSS=1460 SACK_PERM=1 TS
33 39.579735666	93.184.221.39	10.8.2.15	TCP	60 http > 40147 [SYN, ACK] Seq=0 Ack=1 Win=65535 Len=0 MSS=1460
34 39.579863886	10.8.2.15	93.184.221.39	TCP	54 40147 > http [ACK] Seq=1 Ack=1 Win=29200 Len=0

Figure 45: TCP three-way handshake

To start a successful connection between a server and a client, it takes three simple steps: first, the client sends a synchronization [SYN] packet to start a communication; then, the server replies with its own [SYN] and an acknowledgement [ACK] as a confirmation that it has received the [SYN] sent first from the client; and finally, the client replies back with the acknowledgement [ACK] that it has received the [SYN] from the server.

By setting the type of attack to "SSYN" on the MeTus Delphi tool, an attack was carried out on a website for ten seconds. In these ten seconds, from the attacker more than 21,000 TCP packets were sent to the target webserver. Therefore, in a DDoS attack, to calculate the total number of TCP packets sent to a target every ten seconds, the number of bots controlled by the botnet master can be multiplied by approximately 21,000. This shows that a DDoS attack can be more effective than a DoS attack which is carried out by using only one source in disturbing the normal functioning of an online service.

No.	Time	Source	Destination	Protocol	Length	Info
1			74.125.136.147			74 48768 > http [SYN] Seq=0 Win=29200 Len=0 MSS=1460 SACK_PERM=1 TS
2	0.000203000	10.0.2.15	74.125.136.147	TCP		74 48769 > http [SYN] Seq=0 Win=29200 Len=0 MSS=1460 SACK_PERM=1 TS
3	0.000927000	10.0.2.15	74.125.136.147	TCP		74 48770 > http [SYN] Seq=0 Win=29200 Len=0 MSS=1460 SACK_PERM=1 TS
4	0.000995000	10.0.2.15	74.125.136.147	TCP		74 48771 > http [SYN] Seq=0 Win=29200 Len=0 MSS=1460 SACK_PERM=1 TS
5	0.001186000	10.0.2.15	74.125.136.147	TCP		74 48772 > http [SYN] Seq=0 Win=29200 Len=0 MSS=1460 SACK_PERM=1 TS
6	0.001447000	10.0.2.15	74.125.136.147	TCP		74 48773 > http [SYN] Seq=0 Win=29200 Len=0 MSS=1460 SACK_PERM=1 TS
7	0.001879000	10.0.2.15	74.125.136.147	TCP		74 48774 > http [SYN] Seq=0 Win=29200 Len=0 MSS=1460 SACK_PERM=1 TS
8	0.002146000	10.0.2.15	74.125.136.147	TCP		74 48775 > http [SYN] Seq=0 Win=29200 Len=0 MSS=1460 SACK_PERM=1 TS
9	0.002316000	10.0.2.15	74.125.136.147	TCP		74 48776 > http [SYN] Seq=0 Win=29200 Len=0 MSS=1460 SACK_PERM=1 TS
10	0.002476000	10.0.2.15	74.125.136.147	TCP		74 48777 > http [SYN] Seq=0 Win=29200 Len=0 MSS=1460 SACK_PERM=1 TS
11	0.043120000	74.125.136.147	10.0.2.15	TCP		60 http > 48768 [SYN, ACK] Seq=0 Ack=1 Win=65535 Len=0 MSS=1460
12	0.043170000	10.0.2.15	74.125.136.147	TCP		54 48768 > http [ACK] Seq=1 Ack=1 Win=29200 Len=0
13	0.043327000	10.0.2.15	74.125.136.147	TCP		66 [TCP segment of a reassembled PDU]
14	0.043531000	74.125.136.147	10.0.2.15	TCP		60 http > 48768 [ACK] Seq=1 Ack=13 Win=65535 Len=0
15	0.043972000	74.125.136.147	10.0.2.15	TCP		60 http > 48769 [SYN, ACK] Seq=0 Ack=1 Win=65535 Len=0 MSS=1460

Figure 46: Packets captured by Wireshark during SSYN attack

Figure 18, shows how fast the synchronization "[SYN]" TCP packets are sent, even before the server gets a chance to reply to the client with a "[SYN, ACK]" TCP packet confirming that it has received the "[SYN]". In addition, as discussed in part 3.4 DDoS attack using Compromised Hosts, the TCP flooding achieves its target of disrupting the online service by receiving the "[SYN, ACK]" TCP packet from the server. However, the client never sends back the "[ACK]" TCP packet to the server which is waiting to finish the process of creating a connection. This can be seen when analyzing all the captured packets by the Wireshark: There was no "[ACK]" TCP packet sent from the client (10.0.2.15) to the server (74.125.136.147).

34

4 Mitigating DoS and DDoS Attacks

The focus of the past two chapters were DoS and DDoS attacks: the techniques of different tools were discussed and how they are used to attack the server, as well as specifying different attacks such as UDP flooding, TCP flooding and HTTP flooding. At the practical implementation, the server was affected during the HTTP flooding and it was not functional anymore, not even for genuine clients. As long as the attack was taking place the server could not provide the service it was meant to provide to the users.

At this stage of an attack, the company may lose money and the trust of the customers. In general, already the simple threat of a potential DDoS attack can be damaging for an enterprise or organization. Therefore, the responsible staff such as network and web administrators should always be on standby and alert to protect the systems from any outside attack. In this particular case, they are the ones responsible for mitigating DDoS attacks.

Since the time DoS attacks have started to pose a security threat, different fixes from the operating system side as well as defending mechanisms have been applied by different providers. This can be noticed when doing online research on what kind of DoS attacks were a threat at a specific period of time and how they faded out from being a problem after a permanent fix was placed by the different operating system or network hardware producers. However, the success of attackers does not stop there, as they constantly find different vulnerabilities and better ways to carry out DoS and DDoS attacks by using the growth of the Internet and the increase of computation powers of personal computers for their advantage.

Currently, there are many security providers offering network security for companies. In the following paragraph, some of the existing protection mechanisms will be shed light on as examples:

4.1 Iptables

Iptables is a firewall, installed by default on all official Ubuntu distributions (Ubuntu, Kubuntu, Xubuntu). When installing Ubuntu, Iptables is already available, however, by default it is configured to allow all traffic [cf. Help.ubunto.com 2013, n.p.].

The Iptables installed on Ubuntu by default contains three different chains. All three allow the entire traffic incoming and outgoing from the local host, unless the administrator saves some rules and conditions to be checked by the Iptables on the packets involving the host. When typing the command "Iptables –L" as a root user, the three Iptables chains are shown and rules that are put in place by the administrator. Figure 19 shows the three chains of Iptables and the default rules how they are setup. It also shows the rules allowing all the packets emerging from the local host, the packets destined to the local host, and the packets which are not destined for the local host, but which should be forwarded instead by the local host to the right destination.

```
Chain INPUT (policy ACCEPT)
target     prot opt source                    destination

Chain FORWARD (policy ACCEPT)
target     prot opt source                    destination

Chain OUTPUT (policy ACCEPT)
target     prot opt source                    destination
```

Figure 47: Iptables default rules

Below, the three Iptables chains will be discussed:

- **Chain Input:** this chain is directly responsible for handling packets sent to the local host. If the administrator wants to restrict a packet from a certain country, a malicious website or a packet which does not meet certain criteria, the rules under the "Chain INPUT" should be updated or appended.
- **Chain Forward:** in this chain, the packets received are not directly destined for the host which is receiving them; rather, the host receiving the packet is responsible for ensuring that the packets are forwarded to the target host. This chain is mainly applicable for routers installed between two different networks. If a certain IP address or some malicious packet should not reach the target host, a rule can be set under the "Chain FORWARD" to drop the packets.
- **Chain Output:** a rule can be set also for packets going out from the local host to another host. Any restriction made on these packets should be added under the "Chain OUTPUT".

36

4.1.1 Setting up mitigation rules using Iptables on the server

As discussed above, different chains are used in the Iptables to restrict packets emerging from the local host, those destined to the local host, and those packets that are passing through the local host. In a DDoS attack, the traffic mainly causing the disruption of the system is coming from outside. Therefore, the solution for mitigating a DDoS attack mainly lies on the rules that are set under the "Chain INPUT".

Before setting the rules under the Input chain, it is important to check on which interface the rules must be set. In this practical experiment the webserver installed on an Ubuntu client, which is running on a VirtualBox, has two interfaces. The first one is "eth0", which is used to access the Internet, and "eth1" dedicated to listening to requests coming from outside for hosts accessing the webserver. Therefore, all the rules that will be set to protect the webserver from a DDoS attack will be affecting "eth1". After ensuring the interface, it is possible to append the first rule in the Iptables.

iptables -I INPUT -p tcp --dport 80 -i eth1 -m state --state NEW -m recent --set

The above command line was entered into the Ubuntu webserver. This command keeps track of the new hosts connecting to the webserver client. The first part "-I" of the command specifies under which chain the rule will be set, i.e. "INPUT". The second part "-p" specifies the type of protocol "tcp", while "—dport" specifies the port which is listening. Since a webserver is running on the Ubuntu client, the port number "80" is open and listening to any requests coming from outside. The part "--state" is to indicate that the main interest should be a new connection established to the server. The last part of the command line "—-set" is to indicate that the rule is newly set. On the other hand, if the administrator wants to append the rule he/she has to change the "—-set" to "—-update".

iptables -I INPUT -p tcp --dport 80 -i eth0 -m state --state NEW -m recent --update -- seconds 10 --hitcount 10 -j DROP

The rule above is the same as the first command set above, up to the part "—-update". The part "—-seconds" helps to specify the time and to check if a connection has been established before in the specified duration. The next part of the command

"—-hitcount" is to check if a specific IP address has been connected more than the specified count with the time set, in this case the time is 10 seconds. The last part is "DROP", which specifies what the Iptables should do if a specific IP address has tried to connect more than the count entered in the specified time. In general, the purpose of this rule is to check if a specific host has been connected to the server in the last ten seconds more than ten times. If this condition is fulfilled, the Iptables will automatically drop the IP address. In this case, the drop blocks the IP address for two minutes.

4.1.2 Setting up an attack on the server

After having set the rules in the Iptables, the scenario of the DDoS attack in Chapter 2 was repeated. For this test, the attacking speed of the traffic sent to the server on the LOIC tool was set to the maximum. The attack was carried out for ten minutes from the LOIC tool.

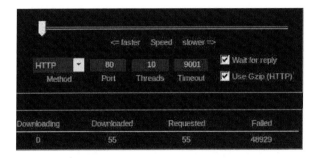

Figure 48: Attack statistics on the LOIC tool

In the ten minutes while the attack was carried out, a screenshot of the statistics in Figure 20 from the LOIC tool was taken. As mentioned above, the speed on the slide bar was set to "faster", the attacking "Method" was set to "HTTP", and "Port" was set to "80" as the target was a webserver. The status bar of the LOIC tool at the bottom shows the number of packets that were sent to flood the webserver. In total, the LOIC tool sent 48.984 packets to the server, out of the 48.984 packets, 55 requests were accepted by the server and downloaded successfully. This can be seen under the "Requested" field on the LOIC tool. The remaining 48.929 HTTP GET packets sent to the server failed automatically. This number is shown on the LOIC tool under the "Failed" field.

Table 1 shows the distribution of the successful packets that reached the server in relation to time. In the first second, from all the packets (approximately 10 packets/sec) ten packets were accepted. Then, for the next two minutes all the packets sent failed to hit the target. After two minutes, the time which is set on the Iptables rule, additional nine packets were successful in reaching the target server. The sequence continued like this during the ten minutes of the attack.

In the first attempt of the LOIC tool attack, ten packets were accepted but after every two minutes, nine more packets were accepted. No explanation was found why in the first attempt one additional packet was accepted by the server, compared to the packets accepted after each two minutes timeout:

Time (in minutes)	Number of hosts accessing server
0 (500ms)	10
2	19
4	28
6	37
8	46
10	55

Table 1: Hosts accessing the server every two minutes

4.1.3 Handling of the attack on the server side

On the server side, no abnormal functionality was shown. A request coming from the server checking the "server status" and all other requests coming from different hosts accessing the webpage, were handled without any delay even if the attack from the LOIC tool was taking place at the same time.

PID	Connections		Threads		Async connections		
	total	accepting	busy	idle	writing	keep-alive	closing
2782	1	yes	1	24	0	0	0
2783	9	yes	9	16	0	1	0
Sum	10		10	40	0	1	0

```
                R        W R  R      R      RRRR R  . . . . . . . . . . . . . .
. . . . . . . . . . . . . . . . . . . . . . . . . . . . . . . . . . . . . . . . . . . . . . . . . . . . . . . . . . . . . . .
. . . . . . . . . . . . . . . . . . . . . .
```

Figure 49: The Apache server handling requests

While the Apache server was handling the genuine traffic coming from different hosts, it was also processing the fake requests sent from the LOIC client, which succeeded to pass the Iptables rules and to reach the webserver. Figure 21 shows how it is handling all requests at the same time. The threads assigned with "R" (Reading Request) are requests coming from the LOIC client. They are occupying the threads only for the timeout of the Apache server for each connection. In this case, the time out is set to one minute. Therefore, every minute the symbolical representation of the threads shown below the table is left only with "W" (Sending Reply) and that is the thread assigned for the local host reading the status of the server.

4.1.4 Denying access to a specific IP address

In the previous part, the Iptables rule set was blocking an IP address for two minutes when the IP address was attempting to send numerous requests within a short period of time. However, there are situations when it is required to deny a complete access from a host, after proving the host is trying to carry out a DDoS attack.

One way to set up the Iptables is to log the requests, which are blocked when they exceed the limit of requests set by the Iptables. In this implementation, all the IP addresses which are making more than ten requests in ten seconds will be blocked. For these blocked packets to be saved by the Iptables in the System Log, the following command was set in the Iptables.

40

iptables -I INPUT 5 -m limit --limit 5/min -j LOG --log-prefix "iptables denied: " --log-level 7

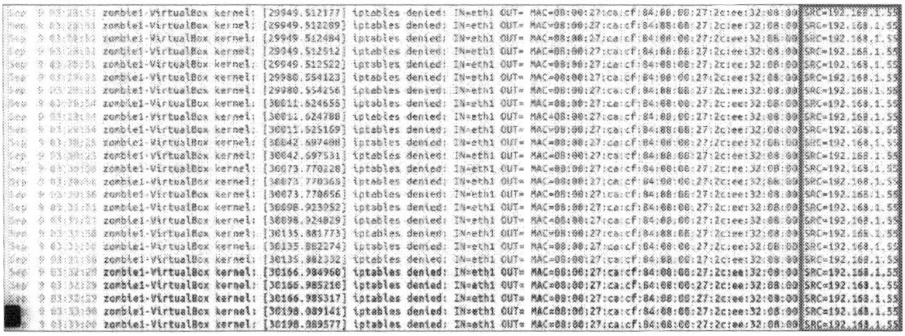

Figure 50: List of packets dropped by the Iptables

Figure 22 shows the list of packets that were blocked by the Iptables. From this table it can be analyzed which IP address has been trying to send too many packets in a short period of time. In this practical experiment, it is easy to see the source IP address "192.168.1.55" marked in the red rectangle which has been attempting to access the server. Therefore, it is easy to identify which IP address needs to be blocked from complete access.

Another way to check which hosts are utilizing the resources of the server is to check by using the "netstat" command.

netstat -ntu | awk '{print $5}' | cut -d: -f1 | sort | uniq -c | sort –n

Entering this command on the terminal of the server gives the result in Figure 23:

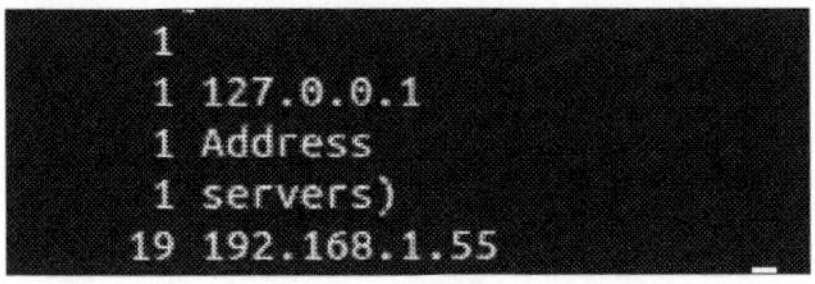

```
1
1 127.0.0.1
1 Address
1 servers)
19 192.168.1.55
```

Figure 51: Using the netstat command to check connections to the server

In Figure 23, one connection from the local host and 19 connections from the client "192.168.1.55" can be seen. In this result it is also possible to see that the client "192.168.1.55" is consuming too many resources. Therefore, it is important to find a permanent solution for this kind of hosts which are trying to disrupt the function of the server. In order to block the IP address, two ways can be used: the first one is by using the Iptables "drop" command and the second one is by downloading "dsniff".

4.1.4.1 Blocking an IP address using Iptables

To block an IP address using the Iptables command is shown below:

iptables -A INPUT -s 192.168.1.55 -j DROP

For this command to take effect in blocking the IP address, the server needs to be restarted, in case the specified IP address is already connected. To ensure the IP address remains blocked, even after the server is restarted and also for all the Iptables rules applied so far to be permanent, these rules need to be saved to a file. The file also needs to be restored by the Iptables every time the server is restarted. This can be handled by the following two commands:

iptables-save   >   /etc/iptables.up.rules
iptables-restore < /etc/iptables.up.rules

4.1.4.2 Blocking an IP address using "dsniff"

The second way to block an IP address without the need to restart the server is to install a tool called "dsniff": *"dsniff is a password sniffer which handles FTP, Telnet, SMTP, HTTP, POP, poppas, NNTP, IMAP, SNMP, LDAP, Rlogin, RIP, OSPF, PPTP MS-CHAP, NFS, VRRP, YP/NIS, SOCKS, X11, CVS, IRC, AIM, ICQ, Napster, PostgreSQL, Meeting Maker, Citrix, ICA, Symantec pcAnywhere, NAI Sniffer, Microsoft SMB, Oracle SQL*Net, Sybase and Microsoft SQL protocols"* [Danielle n.d.].

The "dsniff" package contains many tools for different use, the one tool which is used to block the IP address is TCPKILL. This tool needs only the IP address of the client which will be blocked. The command below can be used to block the attacker:

Tcpkill host 192.168.1.100

42

4.2 The ModSecurity application

ModSecurity is a web application, which a single developer initially started in 2002 as a hobby. Since 2011, it has been owned by Trustwave. *"In today's world, over 70% of all attacks carried out over are done so at the web application level, so we need to implement security at multiple levels, as organizations need all the help they can get in making their systems secure. Web application firewalls are deployed to establish an external security layer that increases security and detects and prevents attacks before they reach the web application. One of the more commonly used application layer firewalls is ModSecurity, which is an open source intrusion detection and prevention system"* [Kumar 2014, n.p.].

ModSecurity can work with Apache, Nginx and IIS. The ModSecurity will be used in the practical implementation in attempt to mitigate the DoS and DDoS attacks demonstrated in Chapter 2 and 3.

4.2.1 Installing ModSecurity

Before starting to install ModSecurity, it is required to install the dependencies *libxml2 libxml2-dev libxml2-utils*. Afterwards, it is possible to install ModSecurity using the command line *apt-get install libapache-mod-security*.

4.2.2 Configuring ModSecurity rules

After installing ModSecurity, some recommended default rules in the configuration file of ModSecurity were set. These included first changing "SecRuleEngine" from "DetectionOnly" to "On", which enabled the rules entered to start monitoring the network. The second setting to update was changing the memory size of "SecRequestBodyLimit" and "SecRequestBodyInMemoryLimit" to limit the size of a file that can be uploaded from a client to a server.

4.2.3 OWASP core rules

The Open Web Application Security Project is a non-profitable organization working for a better protection of any web application. OWASP provides an open source Core Rule Set (CRS) and ModSecurity uses this core set of rules to build its Web Application Firewall (WAF). From the sets of rules OWASP provides for

ModSecurity, some of them are directly used to protect a system from DoS and DDoS:

- HTTP Denial of Service Protections - defense against HTTP Flooding and Slow HTTP DoS Attacks.
- Automation Detection - Detecting bots, crawlers, scanners and other surface malicious activity.
- HTTP Protection - detecting violations of the HTTP protocol and a locally defined usage policy [cf. owasp.org 2014]

After the installation of ModSecurity the CRC with the name "*SpiderLabs-owasp-modsecurity-crs.tar.gz*" was downloaded from the following link:

https://github.com/SpiderLabs/owasp-modsecurity-crs/tarball/master

After unpacking the downloaded file and copying it to the ModSecurity folder, a symbolic link is created to all the activated base rules downloaded. Then, to protect the Apache server, the rules are included in the "modsecurity.conf" of the Apache. This can be done by adding the line "*Include "/etc/modsecurity/activated_rules/*.conf""* at the end of the configuration file.

In one of the steps of setting up the ModSecurity, a considerable amount of time was spent in researching the correct configuration file. In previous versions of Ubuntu, the configuration file for ModSecurity was "*sudo gedit /etc/apache2/mods-available/mod-security.conf* ". In this practical implementation of mitigating a DDoS attack, the latest version Ubuntu 14.04 was used and the configuration file naming was different: The location of the configuration file was the same but the name was changed to "securtiy2.conf". This difference occurs because ModSecurity changes the different file names in different versions. In this case, referring to the documentation of the ModSecurity is recommended.

4.2.4 Finalizing the ModSecurity installation

After all the above steps were done, the Apache server was restarted to reload all the new configurations. To ensure that all the configurations of ModSecurity are set correctly, a simple SQL injection was tested. This test was possible without having to set up any login page. The login page was not required since the request was processed by the ModSecurity and identified as an SQL injection attack. Therefore, the response was sent directly from the ModSecurity, without the request reaching the webserver. The default response of the ModSecurity can be seen in Figure 24.

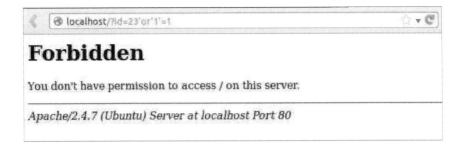

Figure 52: ModSecurity response to SQL injection attack

4.3 The Mod Evasive tool

In the middle of doing research for ModSecurity, some sources were recommending another WAF specialized in protecting a system from HTTP DoS, DDoS and brute force attack called "Mod Evasive". ModSecurity is not directly used to protect a webserver from DoS and DDoS attacks but it fixes many vulnerabilities of applications. This means, it can protect the system indirectly from application exploit denial of service attack and the Mod Evasive can be used especially for HTTP DDoS attacks.

As a first step, Mod Evasive has to be downloaded and installed by following the guide on the website [cf. Thefanclub.co.za 2012, n.p.]. The installation on the website used was set for Ubuntu 12.04 LTS server. However, as already mentioned for this practical implementation Ubuntu 14.04 was used, therefore, in the Mod Evasive downloaded for Ubuntu 14.04, the file naming of the configuration file was changed from "mod-evasive.conf" to "evasive.conf". The content of the "evasive.conf" can be seen in Figure 25:

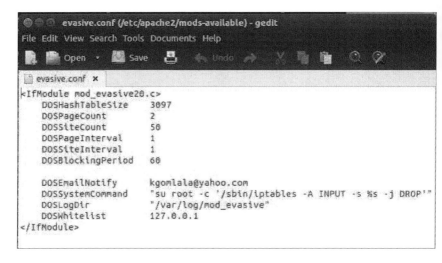

Figure 53: Mod Evasive configuration file content

In the "evasive.conf" file, all the parameters were set to specify in which situations of a DoS attack the system should react and how it should react to the attack. The description of the parameters can be found on the "readme" file downloaded when installing Mod Evasive. Most of the parameters default value was kept the same. Some values were changed to analyze how the Mod Evasive mitigated the attack. The entry for the parameter "DOSBlockingPeriod" is specified in seconds and the default value was "10". This was changed to "60", in order to have more time to check if the attacker was presented with an "access denied" message. The next value changed was "DOSSystemCommand", the Iptables "INPUT" rule was used to block the IP address of the attacker. Then, the "DOSEmailNotify" entry was changed to a private email, but unfortunately, no email was received. The settings for an email to be sent are different depending on the respective versions of Ubuntu.

The "DOSLogDir" specifies the directory where the log should be saved. During the attack a log was saved successfully in the directory with the name "DOS <IP address>". This can be seen in Figure 26:

```
root@zombie1-VirtualBox:/var/log/mod_evasive# ls
dos-192.168.1.55
```

Figure 54: Mod Evasive tool DoS attack log

During the attack the usage of the resources of the server was monitored by using the Glances tool. At the beginning of the attack the CPU usage was rising up to 47.3%. After the Mod Evasive started taking defensive measures, the CPU usage percentage started to decrease and after three seconds it was back to the normal usage percentage.

4.4 The Snort intrusion detection tool

Snort is an intrusion detection tool, which is based on rules saved in its configuration. The rules are made depending on the signature of the virus or on a unique content, which can be found in the packet. Most of the time, IDS systems such as Snort are placed behind the router or firewall. Usually, an intrusion detection system captures data from the network and applies its rules to that data to detect anomalies in the packet [cf. Rehman 2003, p.5].

To apply Snort in the system used for the practical implementation, it was required to include a rule which could be applied to the incoming data. Therefore, this required making a rule that was specifically designed to identify the packets sent by the attacker to flood the system and cause a denial of service attack. In order to write the log or alert rule, the Wireshark network utility tool was used to sniff the packets coming into the network and analyze the difference that could be seen between a packet coming from a genuine user and a packet coming from the attacker. The general difference of the two packets was shown in Chapter 2.6: Figure 2 was showing the request sent from a genuine user and Figure 9 the random request generated by the LOIC tool. It is easy to notice the size difference between the two packets. However, writing a Snort rule requires analyzing the packets in detail.

```
▶ GET / HTTP/1.1\n
  Accept: */*\n
  User-Agent: Mozilla/4.0 (compatible; MSIE 7.0; Windows NT 6.0)\n
  Accept-Encoding: gzip, deflate\n
  Host: 192.168.1.100\n
  \n
  [Full request URI: http://192.168.1.100/]
  [HTTP request 1/1]
0040  b5 cf 47 45 54 20 2f 20  48 54 54 50 2f 31 2e 31   ..GET /  HTTP/1.1
0050  0d 41 63 63 65 70 74 3a  20 2a 2f 2a 0a 55 73 65   .Accept:  */*.Use
0060  72 2d 41 67 65 6e 74 3a  20 4d 6f 7a 69 6c 6c 61   r-Agent:  Mozilla
```

Figure 55: LOIC GET request content from Wireshark tool

Figure 27 shows the content of the GET request coming from the LOIC tool, which differs from the request coming from other request sent by genuine clients. In general, the GET request coming from a genuine client is "GET /HTTP/1.1\r\n", but in this case the GET request coming from the LOIC tool was "GET /HTTP/1.1\n". Therefore, this means the content of these two requests was also different and this was used to make the Snort rule, which alerts the system administrator whenever there is such kind of DoS attack coming from a client. The Snort rule made using this condition is the following:

alert tcp $EXTERNAL_NET any -> $HOME_NET $HTTP_PORTS (msg:"LOIC DoS attacking Tool"; flow: established,to_server; content:"|47 45 54 20 2f 20 48 54 54 50 2f 31 2e 31 0a|"; threshold: type threshold, track by_src, count 10 , seconds 10; sid:1234569;)

The Snort rule above contains different parts:

- The beginning of the rule is "alert": this can be changed to "log", if the administrator prefers to save the attack into a log file, rather than getting an alert to his/ her email address. Then, the rule specifies the packet type.
- The source IP address and port, which consider all incoming traffic from any IP address and any port; the destination IP address can be destined to any host, however, the port number should be sent only to "$HTTP_PORTS" .
- The message "msg" part contains the text "LOIC DoS attacking Tool " that will be sent or logged when there is an attack coming from a LOIC tool.

48

- The "flow" allows rules to only apply to traffic flowing to the server and the connection must be fully established.
- The "content" allows the administrator to put a specific content from the packet payload. From this, Snort can trigger an alert or log to notify the system administrator.
- The "threshold" is to specify a threshold that must be exceeded before a Snort rule triggers an alert or a log. In this rule the threshold is the following: if the number of requests sent from a single source exceeds ten within ten seconds, the notification is triggered.
- The "sid" is a unique Snort identification for a specific rule.

As it can be seen, the rule above did not directly take measures to mitigate the DoS or DDoS attack. However, Snort can be handy in notifying the responsible party, so that extra measures can be taken to mitigate the attack. Snort can be used in combination with the tools explained in Chapter 4.1 and 4.3.

4.5 Additional Dos and DDoS mitigation mechanisms

In this Chapter, four different mechanisms of mitigations are discussed. Many organizations and private firms use different ways and software to secure their systems and to safely mitigate DoS and DDoS attacks targeting their systems. Below, three different commonly used mechanisms to protect online services are discussed.

4.5.1 CloudFlare and Incapsula

One of the security network operators and software fighting online attacks currently present in the market and commonly used by enterprises all over the world is called CloudFlare. CloudFlare is an American IT security company founded in 2009, which offers its services to mitigate the risk of online threats, including DoS attacks, and to generally improve the security of websites [cf. CloudFlare.com, n.d.].

Another application delivery service, which can, among others, be used to mitigate DDoS attacks on Layer 7, is Incapsula, a subsidiary of the American data security company Imperva. As described on its website, *"Incapsula protects applications and infrastructure against all types of DDoS threats. These include network-based attacks (e.g. Slowloris, ICMP or TCP & UDP floods) as well as application layer attacks (e.g. GET flood) that attempt to overwhelm server resources. Supporting Unicast and Anycast technologies, the service leverages a many-to-many defense methodology, automatically detecting and mitigating advanced DDoS attacks that exploit application and Web server vulnerabilities, hit-and-run DDoS events, and large botnets"* [Incapsula 2014, n.p.].

Both, Incapsula and CloudFlare provide their service starting from free up to "enterprise level" by charging fees for their service.

In normal scenarios when a request comes from a client to a webserver, the request reaches the server directly passing through the network and transport devices found in-between. The manner, in which both CloudFlare and Incapsula improve the security of the webserver, is by acting as a proxy between the web hosting server and the client accessing the website. This is made possible by changing the DNS settings and routing the traffic through Incapsula's or CloudFlare's network, rather than directly reaching the webserver. This rerouting of the traffic through these services, gives them the right to inspect the packets which are passing through. Therefore, they can apply all their checks to the packets and decide whether the packet is safe to pass it to the destination IP address or whether to drop the packet if it is perceived as a threat.

4.5.2 Software and hardware load balancer

A load balancer is a system placed before the servers to handle all the traffic coming from outside and distributing the workload to the different systems, which are capable of processing the incoming request. Load balancer protects a server from a SYN flooding attack by passing the client to the server after the full TCP handshake is completed.

Through time *"the term Load Balancing switch has become antiquated and is being steadily replaced with the term Application Delivery Controller (ADC). The ADC's have additional features not found in older load balancing technologies such as content manipulation, advanced routing strategies as well as highly configurable server health monitoring"* (Davis 2010, p. 4].
The modern load balancer ADC gives protection to the server from application layer DDoS attacks. For example, the Slowloris tool carries out a DoS attack by consuming a connection by holding it for a long time and by feeding an HTTP

header to a server in an extremely slow fashion. The ADC takes the load from the server by passing the packet only when it receives the final double carriage that indicates the end of the header from the client. However, the Slowloris does not send the double carriage. Therefore, the ADC discards the packet before it reaches the server.

4.5.3 CAPTCHA authentication

In the discussion of Chapter 2 and 3, the different tools used to carry out a DoS and DDoS attack were shed light on. All the attacking tools were generating random packets to flood the target server. This can have an advantage in protecting a system from such attacks. It can be seen in many websites when a log in fails more than a certain amount of times (e.g. on the Yahoo website), it presents the user with obscured letters or numbers in attempt to distinguish, if the user who is trying to log in is a real person or machine generated.

If a server with CAPTCHA (Completely Automated Public Turing test to tell Computers and Humans Apart) is placed between the webserver and the outside user, the CAPTCHA can limit all the packets generated by DDoS tools from reaching the webserver, since there is no way for the randomly generated packets by the attacking tools to solve the presented word puzzle. An example CAPTCHA can be seen in Figure 28.

Figure 56: A Yahoo CAPTCHA authentication

This solution presented here does not only have advantages. One of the disadvantages is that running the CAPTCHA service would also require its own resource like CPU and memory. One solution for this problem would be to set a threshold for the load on the webserver, and when the workload on the server passes this threshold, the server should activate the CAPTCHA service suspecting that it is under attack. Again, when the load on the webserver is less than the threshold, the web server can turn back to the normal status by deactivating the CAPTCHA service. This means that the resource, which was assigned for the CAPTCHA, can be utilized by the webserver in normal situations. Using CAPTCHA can be effective especially when it comes to application layer DoS and DDoS attacks.

5 Conclusion

In Chapter 1, a background on the evolvement of DoS and DDoS attacks is given. This included an overview of the different types of attacks used by hacktivist groups and their motivations behind. It is shown that there are different categories of attacks, classified by the respective layers of the network which are targeted for an attack.

This overview is followed by an analysis of existing challenges in order to defend a system from a DoS or DDoS attack. It is shown that the common existing infrastructures such as routers and firewalls are not capable of protecting the system alone. Therefore, it can be said that it is necessary to complement these infrastructures with additional software and hardware for mitigating such attacks. In the part on the state of the art, currently available mechanisms to mitigate a DoS and DDoS attack are discussed.

In Chapter 2 an attack scenario is created by using different hosts or clients installed on a virtual machine. The practical implementation contains an attacker, a server and a normal user. The attacker is carrying out the attack by using a LOIC tool. The server is running an Apache 2 web server providing access to a webpage created for this practical application. The normal user is created to access the normal website provided by the server.

During the practical application, an HTTP flood attack is carried out by the LOIC tool on the Apache 2 server installed. The Apache Server is showing the effect from the attack and it is not responsive for all the requests coming. As a result, the attack is captured by a network analyzing tool and the difference between the requests sent from the LOIC tool and the normal user is compared. By using the difference as a bouncing board, a Snort rule is made in order to mitigate the attack.

Chapter 3 looks at the creation of a botnet. For this purpose, a MeTus Delphi tool is installed on the side of the attacker and at the same time, all the requested steps such as setting up DUC and PortForwarding are implemented. After this process, it is possible to create a virus which opens a backdoor on the victim's computer and thereby compromises the client to become part of the botnet. By using the compromised clients a SSYN attack is carried out. Again by using the network utility tool, it is described how the MeTus Delphi tool uses the vulnerability of the TCP three-way handshake to carry out an attack.

Chapter 4 deals with available mitigation mechanisms to protect a server against DoS and DDoS attacks. The existing mechanisms such as Iptables, ModSecurity, Mod Evasive, Snort and other third party companies providing mitigation are described. By analyzing these mechanisms, it is shown how they can be adapted to mitigate certain types of DoS and DDoS attacks.

It is demonstrated when mitigating DoS and DDoS attacks by using different tools, that each of them is using its own techniques to detect an attack. In other words, each tool can only mitigate a certain kind of attack. Therefore, in order to increase the security level to a maximum, it is recommended to use the mentioned mitigation techniques in combination.

In addition, the practical application shows that the tools such as Iptables, ModSecurity, and Mod Evasive are detecting an attack by using the IP address of a host by counting how many times the host sends a request in a specific period of time. These tools, however, can be vulnerable when they are attacked by a botnet which contains thousands of hosts. A reason for this is that the attacker does not need to use a single IP address multiple times in a short period of time. Again, this risk of an attack is minimized by using a combination of mitigation techniques.

The challenges encountered while trying to implement the practical application are the following: a first obstacle is the lack of adequate documents explaining the different attacking tools. Even when they are found after researching, the download links referred to are already deleted or blocked due to sensitivity reasons. This hinders a smooth implementation of the practical application considerably. This problem is solved by taking the risk to download the tools from unsafe websites.

Another obstacle is encountered when trying to simulate the real world attack since virtual machines are used instead of a real work environment. This means that it is hard to rely on the results stemming from the practical application.

The following open questions remain: Additional research and tests should be undertaken by security experts, in order to get a better understanding of the different forms of attacks. Attention should be drawn to the fact that DoS and DDoS attacks are still advancing and constantly adapting to bypass the existing mitigation techniques.

It is recommended that enterprises and organizations always perform tests against their own systems to check how far their systems are capable of handling a potential DoS and DDoS attack rather than reacting only when already under attack. This can prevent from considerable harm to the company, not only from a financial perspective, but also regarding customers' trust.

6 Bibliography

[Arbor Networks 2011a]. Arbor Networks: Layered Intelligent DDoS Mitigation Systems. Why Internet Service providers are in a unique position to deliver layered DDoS attack protection services. White paper, Massachusetts, 2011a. In: http://www.arbornetworks.com/ddos/Layered%20Intelligent%20DDoS%20Mitigation%20Systems.pdf [date: 09/06/2014].

[Arbor Networks 2011b]. Arbor Networks: The Growing Threat of Application-Layer DDoS Attacks. How Peakflow® SP can help Service Providers Protect Critical Carrier Services and Customers. White paper, Massachusetts, 2011b. In: http://www.arbornetworks.com/component/docman/doc_download/467-the-growing-threat-of-application-layer-ddos-attacks?Itemid=442. [date: 09/06/2014].

[Capers 2013]. Capers, Zach: The Fraud Examiner. The Evolving Threat of DDoS Attacks. Austin, 2013. In: http://www.acfe.com/fraud-examiner.aspx?id=4294976615 [date: 08/06/2014].

[CloudFlare.com, n.d.]. CloudFlare.com: CloudFlare security. CloudFlare Inc., Delaware, 2012. In: https://www.cloudflare.com/features-security [date: 24/08/2014]

[Danielle n.d.]. Danielle, Lora: Introduction to dsniff. SANS Security Essentials (GSEC) v.1.2e, Global Information Assurance Certification Paper, SANS Institute, n.p., 2000-2002. In: http://www.giac.org/paper/gsec/810/introduction-dsniff/101714 [date: 14/09/2014].

[Davis 2010]. Davis, Brough: Leveraging the Load Balancer to Fight DDoS. SANS Institute, n.p., 2010. In: http://www.sans.org/reading-room/whitepapers/firewalls/leveraging-load-balancer-fight-ddos-33408 [date: 10/09/2014].

[Defense.net 2014]. defense.net: DDoS Attack Timeline, The History & Changing Nature of DDoS Attacks. Belmont, California, 2014. In: http://www.defense.net/ddos-attack-timeline.html [date: 22/06/2014].

[Digitalattackmap.com 2014]. digitalattackmap.com: Powered by Google Ideas. DDoS data ©2013, Arbor Networks, Inc. In: http://www.digitalattackmap.com [date: 22/06/2014].

[Fry 2014]. Fry, Maddy: Anonymous Launches New Cyberattack Against Israel. Time Magazine online edition, 7 April 2014. In: http://time.com/51616/anonymous-israel-attack [date: 20/06/2014].

[Help.ubuntu.com 2013]. Help.ubuntu.com: IptablesHowTo, 2013. In: https://help.ubuntu.com/community/IptablesHowTo [date: 10/09/2014].

[Janssen 2010-2014a]. Janssen, Cory: Three-Way-Handshake. Techopedia, Janalta Interactive Inc., 2010-2014a. In: http://www.techopedia.com/definition/10339/three-way-handshake [date: 20/06/2014].

[Janssen 2010-2014b]. Janssen, Cory: Application Layer. Techopedia, Janalta Interactive Inc., 2010-2014b. In: http://www.techopedia.com/definition/6006/application-layer [date: 20/06/2014].

[Kostadinov 2013]. Kostadinov, Dimitar: Layer Seven DDoS Attacks. InfoSec Institute, Cary, North Carolina, 2013. In: http://resources.infosecinstitute.com/layer-seven-ddos-attacks/ [date: 20/06/2014].

[Kumar 2014]. Kumar, Nikhil: Configuring the ModSecurity Firewall with OWASP Rules, InfoSec Institute, Illinois,18th July 2014. In: http://resources.infosecinstitute.com/configuring-modsecurity-firewall-owasp-rules/ [date: 10/09/2014].

[Les 2013]. Les: HTTP GET Flood DDoS Attack, aka HTTP Object Request Flood. Neustar, 11 July 2013. In: http://www.ddosattacks.biz/attacks/http-post-flood-ddos-attack-definition-mitigation/ [date: 20/06/2014].

[McCarty 2011]. McCarty, Brad: CloudFlare: A website security product accidentally makes sites 60% faster. 7 June 2011, n.p. In: http://thenextweb.com/insider/2011/06/07/cloudflare-a-website-security-product-accidentally-makes-sites-60-faster/ [date: 24/08/2014]

[Noip.com 2014]. No-IP.com: Vitalwerks Internet Solutions, LLC, Nevada, 2014. In: http://www.noip.com/download?page=win [date: 06/09/2014].

[OConnor 2011]. OConnor, TJ: The Jester Dynamic: A Lesson in Asymmetric Unmanaged Cyber Warfare. N.p, 30 December 2011. In: http://www.sans.org/reading-room/whitepapers/attacking/jester-dynamic-lesson-asymmetric-unmanaged-cyber-warfare-33889 [date: 22/06/2014].

[OSCE 2013]. Organization for Security and Co-operation in Europe, Permanent Council Decision No. 1106, 975th Plenary Meeting, Vienna, 3 December 2013. In: http://www.osce.org/pc/109168?download=true [date: 07/09/2014].

[Owasp.org 2014]. Owasp.org: Category:OWASP ModSecurity Core Rule Set Project, OWASP, Maryland, 2014. In: https://www.owasp.org/index.php/Category:OWASP_ModSecurity_Core_Rule_Set_Project [date: 10/09/2014].

[Oxid.it 2009]. Oxid.it: Massimiliano Montoro, Italy, 2001-2009. In: http://www.oxid.it/ca_um/ [date: 06/09/2014].

[PortForward 2014]. PortForward.com: Portforward, LLC, Oregon, 2014. In: http://portforward.com/help/portforwarding.htm [date: 06/09/2014].

[Radware 2013a]. Radware Ltd.: DDoSpedia. N.p., 2013. In: http://security.radware.com/knowledge-center/DDoSPedia/udp-flood/ [date: 20/06/2014].

[Radware 2013b]. Radware Ltd.: Kenig, Ronen/ Manor, Deborah/ Gadot, Ziv/ Trauner, Daniel: DDoS Survival Handbook. Tel Aviv, Israel. 2013. In: http://security.radware.com/uploadedFiles/Resources_and_Content/DDoS_Handbook/DDoS_Handbook.pdf [date: 22/06/2014].

[Ranjan et al. 2006]. Ranjan, Supranamaya/ Swaminathan, Ram/ Uysal, Mustafa/ Knightly, Edward: DDoS-Resilient Scheduling to Counter Application Layer Attacks under Imperfect Detection. In: INFOCOM 2006. 25th IEEE International Conference on Computer Communications. Proceedings 2006, p.1-13.

[Rehman 2003]. Rehman, Rafeeq Ur: Intrusion detection systems with Snort. Prentice Hall PTR, New Jersey, 2003. In:

http://ptgmedia.pearsoncmg.com/images/0131407333/downloads/0131407333.pdf [date: 10/09/2014].

[Shatz 2014]. Shatz, Gur: DDoS attacks in 2014: Smarter, bigger, faster, stronger. Venture Beat News, 20 April 2014. In: http://venturebeat.com/2014/04/20/ddos-attacks-in-2014-smarter-bigger-faster-stronger/ [date: 20/06/2014].

[Spy-emergency 2011]. Spy-emergency.com: NETGATE Technologies, Slovakia 2011. In: http://www.spy-emergency.com/research/malware-database/metus-delphi-28exe-metus-delphi-28-trojanwin32agent.html [date: 06/09/2014].

[TheFanClub.co.za 2012]. TheFanClub.co.za: How to install apache2 mod_security and mod_evasive on Ubuntu 12.04 LTS server. The Fan Club dynamic design solutions, The Fan Club 2001-2014, South Africa. In: http://www.thefanclub.co.za/how-to/how-install-apache2-modsecurity-and-modevasive-ubuntu-1204-lts-server [date: 06/09/2014].

[White House 2011]. White House: International Strategy For Cyberspace. Prosperity, Security and Openness in a Networked World. Washington, May 2011. In: http://www.whitehouse.gov/sites/default/files/rss_viewer/international_strategy_for_cyberspace.pdf [date: 06/08/2014].

[Zannier 2014]. Zannier, Lamberto: Cyber/ICT Security: Building Confidence. In: Security Community, The OSCE Magazine, Vienna, Issue 2, 2014, p. 4-5. In: http://www.osce.org/home/122525?download=true#page=4 [date: 07/09/2014].

27715813R00042

Printed in Great Britain
by Amazon